WOMEN IN THE RENAISSANCE

BY KATHLEEN SIMPSON

TABLE OF CONTENTS

INTRODUCTION

The Renaissance (REH-nih-zahns) was a time of great change in Europe. New ideas took root in Italy during the mid-1300s and spread throughout Europe. Because life changed so much during these years, historians named the period *Renaissance*, a French word that means "rebirth."

Before the Renaissance, much of life focused on religious beliefs. Church leaders were very powerful. They controlled what people could do, think, or learn. A group of scholars disagreed with the church's beliefs. These scholars were known as **humanists**.

Humanists studied the art, books, and buildings of ancient Greece and Rome. They were looking for lost knowledge. The result was a period of learning and change that touched the lives of men and women.

The Renaissance did not affect women as much as men. Still, women were important to society and had many roles to play. They lived and worked on farms, in towns, in churches, and at the courts of royal families.

▲ The Renaissance began in Italy and then spread to the rest of Europe.

Some women studied the natural world and contributed to science. As you read, imagine what these women's lives were like. Picture the world of farmers' wives, queens, and artists during the Renaissance.

◀ Women worked as midwives in the Renaissance.

WOMEN OF THE
WORKING
CLASS

The lives of working women in the Renaissance, especially those on farms and in small villages, remained the same as it had always been. Raising children and taking care of the household were working women's main duties.

Women were largely under the control of their fathers or husbands. By law, husbands could punish their wives for being disobedient. Among women, widows enjoyed the most freedom.

▲ This detail from a painting by the Limbourg brothers shows women gathering hay for a June harvest.

Widows ran the house and often continued to run the family farm or business after a husband had died.

Education

There was no formal education for working-class or poor families. Girls learned at home. They learned how to spin wool, weave cloth, and make clothing. Mothers taught daughters to care for livestock and to make cheese, bread, beer, and wine. They showed their daughters how to cook and use wild plants to make medicines. Girls learned skills they would need for a life as a wife.

For a girl who lived in a town, life was different. A growing number of town families had money for things beyond the basics of food and shelter. If she were lucky, a girl might

▲ Daughters learned all the skills they needed to run a household from their mothers.

attend school, but it would be a school for girls only.

Some wealthy families hired **tutors** to come into their homes and teach their children. Girls studied religion, reading, and sometimes even math. Some learned about the family business. Most also learned housekeeping skills, much like girls in the country.

Girls of the Renaissance married young—most were still in their teens. They usually lived with their parents until marriage. When the time came for a young girl to marry, she did not choose her own husband. The bride and groom might know each other, but their parents arranged the marriage. Parents wanted a marriage that would give their daughters a safe and comfortable home for life.

The groom, in turn, received a **dowry**. A dowry is cash, land, or goods used to help the couple start out in life. The bride's family paid the dowry. The better a girl's dowry was, the stronger her parents' bargaining position would be in choosing a husband for her.

HISTORICAL PERSPECTIVE

Renaissance weddings were much like modern weddings. There was a church service and an exchange of rings, followed by a feast, or reception. At Renaissance weddings, guests brought

crackers. They stacked the crackers in a huge pile. The married couple stood on opposite sides of the pile and tried to kiss over the crackers. This practice evolved into the modern tall wedding cake in use today.

Fathers with money tried to marry their daughters into royal families. A marriage like this would enhance the social position of a wealthy middle-class family.

Sometimes the system of paying a dowry could bankrupt a family. Many girls left home to earn their own living.

Girls from small villages often had to move to larger towns to find work. There, they found jobs as household servants or were hired as **apprentices** (ah-PREHN-tih-sihs). An apprentice works at a craftsperson's shop and learns a trade. These working women did not receive the same wages as men did. Some only earned food and a place to sleep. Others received very low wages.

▲ This 16th-century woodcut shows a bell-maker's workshop.

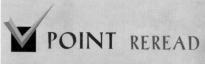 POINT REREAD

Reread pages 4–6. What career choices were available to working-class women of the Renaissance?

Family Life

In the working-class world of the Renaissance, families did chores together. On farms, women worked in the fields, prepared food, or tended livestock. Children worked alongside their parents. Older children often cared for younger ones so that mothers could focus on other tasks. Many women worked to earn extra money.

They did spinning or weaving for other people.

For farm families, Renaissance life was hard. Illness and accidents were common. Average life spans for both men and women were short—between thirty and forty years.

In towns, too, married women worked alongside their husbands. The wife of a skilled craftsperson might learn her husband's craft so she could help out in his shop. She might also do bookkeeping or assist customers.

◀ **This 15th century painting shows a family at work in a shop.**

Some women had their own businesses, making beer, running shops, or washing clothes.

With money of their own, women were an important part of society. They bought goods and gave money to churches and charities.

Childbirth

Motherhood consumed a lot of time for women of all classes in the Renaissance. It was the wife's responsibility to feed, clothe, and educate her children. Many women became pregnant every two years or so. It was common for a woman to have eight or more children. But only a few of them survived. Disease and unhealthy living conditions killed many children when they were young.

PRIMARY SOURCE

A female servant who lived in England in the 1300s complained about her heavy workload:

"I must learn to spin, to reke, to card, to knit, to wash buckets, and by handle, to brew, bake, make mault, reap, bind sheaves, weed in the garden, milke, serve hoggs, make cleane their houses, within doores make beddes, sweep filthy houses, rubbe dirty faggess, beat out old coverlettes, draw up old holes: Then to the kitchen, turne the spit; then scour pottes, wash dishes, fetch in wood, make a fire, scalde milk panes, wash the chare and butter dishes, ring out the cheese clote, set everything in good order."

Most people felt that all women should be married. However, some women stayed single because they did not have dowries. Many others made different choices. Those women who did not marry had a few options available to them. They could go to a large city and find work spinning, weaving, or sewing. Or, they could become nuns. It was common for girls without dowries to become nuns. The Roman Catholic Church was a large part of life for people in Renaissance Europe.

ITS A FACT

A spinster is someone who spins wool into yarn. In the 1600s, so many single women were spinsters that the word took on a new meaning. *Spinster* came to mean "a woman who hasn't married, although she is beyond the usual age for marriage." The word is still used today.

15th century ▶
French painting
of a woman spinning

Catherine of Siena was born a member of the lower middle class. Her father, a tradesperson, dyed clothes. Catherine became a layperson in the Catholic Church. This meant that she had special religious training.

Catherine spent much of her life caring for the sick and the poor. She also wrote letters to important people of the time. These letters expressed her opinions.

Catherine lived in a time when leaders of the Roman Catholic Church were divided. These church leaders couldn't even agree on who should be the **pope**. Catherine wrote many letters to Pope Gregory XI. She felt that he moved too slowly to bring church leaders together. In her letters, she told the pope he was being irresponsible.

PRIMARY SOURCE

This is part of a letter Catherine of Siena wrote, scolding Pope Gregory XI as if he were a misbehaving child.

"Pursue and finish with true holy zeal what you have begun by holy intent. Delay no longer, for your delaying has already been the cause of a lot of trouble. . . . Up, father! No more irresponsibility!"

▲ The Catholic Church named Catherine a saint after she died.

WOMEN OF THE RULING CLASS

A map of 14th century Europe does not look like a modern map. Europe was made up of many small **city-states**. These were ruled by rich, powerful families. Italy, was made up of many such city-states. Wealthy families ruled most of them.

Life in one of these families was not like life on a farm. Girls born into the ruling class learned at home from tutors, many of whom were humanists.

◀ Queen Elizabeth I of England

Humanist tutors taught their female students to read classical books and study ancient art. Daughters of the ruling class also learned to write, paint, and play musical instruments.

This map shows some of ▶ the city-states that existed during the Renaissance.

ITALY

MODENA
MONTEERRAT   MANTUA
SAVOY
MILAN   REPUBLIC OF VENICE
FERRARA
LUCCA
REPUBLIC OF   Florence
SALUZZO   FLORENCE
THE
PAPAL
STATES   Adriatic
Sea
REPUBLIC
OF GENOA   SIENNA
Rome
Naples
Tyrrhenian   KINGDOM
Sea
OF THE
Ionian
Sea
TWO
Mediter   Palermo
SICILIES
ranean Sea

THEY MADE A DIFFERENCE

In 1423, a famous humanist named Vittorino da Feltre (vee-toh-REE-noh FEHL-tray) opened a school in the Italian city-state of Mantua (MAHN-shoo-wuh). A wealthy family supported Vittorino's school. Girls and boys studied there, and so did children from poor families. His students learned to play sports, as well as such subjects as religion and math.

◀ During the Renaissance, there were no government-sponsored schools like there are today.

Marriage and Royal Duties

Like working-class women, girls of the ruling class had no choice about whom they married. Parents made **marriage contracts** for their daughters with other rulers or wealthy, powerful families. These contracts often built bonds between countries.

Parents made the agreements when their daughters were still young. It was common for a girl from a ruling class family to be engaged at age three or four.

What would happen if a girl did not want the marriage her parents had arranged? The law was not on her side. If she married someone else without her parents' consent, that marriage was not legal.

Some arranged marriages turned out well, but others did not work out. When Isabella of France was a baby, her parents arranged for her to marry Edward II of England. Everyone hoped that the marriage would end years of war between the two countries. Isabella married Edward when she was twelve.

◀ Isabella of France

The marriage ended when Isabella's army attacked Edward's. In the end, Isabella took the English throne for her eldest son.

A few girls took on huge duties when they were still very young. For example, Jadwiga (YAHD-vee-gah) of Poland was a child king.

They named her king to make it clear that no one would rule for her. She was crowned at the age of eleven and grew up to be a beloved ruler of Poland. She cared deeply for the poor and sick and founded hospitals and universities.

ITS A FACT

Dowries put a strain on the finances of both rich and poor families. Powerful men in the city-state of Florence had a special investment fund to help pay for their daughters' dowries. In 1480, about one-fifth of all wealthy fathers in Florence participated in the *monte delle doti* (dowry mountain).

◄ **After she died, the Catholic Church named Jadwiga a saint.**

Men of the ruling class spent a great deal of time away from home. Some were soldiers or traders who traveled on business. Others improved their social status by living at court. This meant that they traveled to the homes, or courts, of wealthy ruling families. They lived there and attended social functions. This way, they got to meet many powerful people. Other men managed businesses in other parts of the world. While they were away, wives, mothers, daughters, and sisters took over their duties.

Most rulers were men. In rare cases, women **inherited** the crown because there were no male heirs. Most countries would not allow women to rule. There were a few exceptions. Elizabeth I of England was one of them.

ITS A FACT

England's Elizabeth I inherited the crown after her brother and sister died. Elizabeth lived a long life but never married. She knew that if she did, she would have to turn over much of her power to her husband. Queen Elizabeth I ruled for forty-five years.

◀ Under Elizabeth I's rule, England grew to be a mighty world power.

Women also ruled as **regents**, or substitutes, for young sons and sick husbands. Margaret I of Denmark was a regent. When Margaret's son, Olaf, became king of both Denmark and Norway, Margaret ruled for him. When Olaf died as a teenager, Margaret continued to rule both Denmark and Norway. Then, in 1389, Swedish heads of state asked her to rule their country as well. She did, until her death in 1412.

◀ Margaret I of Denmark

Patrons of the Arts

Europe's ruling class helped spread knowledge during the Renaissance. Both men and women became **patrons** of the arts. Patrons were wealthy people who hired artists, writers, and musicians. The system of patronage allowed patrons to fill their lives and homes with fine things. Having a powerful patron was good for an artist's career. It meant that an artist's work would be popular and in demand.

Isabella d'Este (DEHS-tay) ruled as regent for both her husband and son. She was also a leading patron of the arts. She invited talented artists, writers, and scholars to visit her court. Sometimes she paid for their food and lodging while they visited. At other times, she hired them to create works of art for her. Famous painters and writers visited Isabella's court.

▲ Isabella d'Este hired famous painter Titian (TY-shuhn) to do this portrait of her in 1536.

▲ People at court regularly gathered for parties and social events. There the greatest artists and scholars of the day discussed ideas.

THEY MADE A DIFFERENCE

Catherine de' Medici (MEH-dee-chee) grew up in a powerful and rich family. She was born in Italy in 1519. She was the daughter of a duke and a princess. Pope Clement VII was her uncle. Catherine married a member of the royal family of France when she was fourteen years old. Later, her husband Henry became king of France. Catherine became queen.

Henry and Catherine were well known for their support of the arts. When her husband died in 1559, Catherine ruled as regent for her young son. Catherine hired architects to add to her palace. That palace is now the famous Louvre (LOOV) Museum in Paris.

▲ This is the Louvre today. Catherine de' Medici added the wing now known as the Denon Wing and the Tuileries Gardens.

WOMEN IN THE ARTS AND SCIENCES

Artists of the Renaissance often traveled to other cities to study with famous artists. Part of their training was drawing, sculpting, or painting nude figures. The idea of females painting naked men was unacceptable at the time. People thought that women should paint pictures of nature or family life—if they were allowed to paint at all.

Renaissance women artists and writers were usually the children of artists or writers. Their fathers trained them, sometimes breaking rules so that their daughters could learn the craft.

Marietta Tintoretto (tihn-tuh-REH-toh) was the daughter of a famous artist, Jacopo Tintoretto. Her father wanted her to get a proper artist's training. He dressed her as a boy. As an adult, Marietta worked in her father's studio. She specialized in painting portraits.

Her painting style was so like her father's that people could not tell their work apart. Then, while she was still a young woman, Marietta died in childbirth.

◀ self-portrait of Renaissance artist Artemisia Gentileschi

▲ For hundreds of years, people thought Marietta Tintoretto's famous father painted this painting. Experts now believe that Marietta painted *Portrait of an Old Man with Boy*.

THEY MADE A DIFFERENCE

Elena Cornaro Piscopia (kor-NAHR-oh pees-COH-pee-ah) grew up in Venice, Italy. In 1678, she became the first woman to earn a university doctorate degree. She received a doctorate in philosophy from the University of Padua.

Work and Marriage

Many women of the Renaissance stopped writing or painting when they married. This is one reason we don't know much about female writers and artists of the Renaissance. They didn't write or paint long enough to create a large body of work.

An artist named Sofonisba Anguissola (soh-foh-NEES-bah ahng-GWEE-shoh-lah) was an exception. She painted for most of her long life. In 1560, she served as a painter at the court of Philip II of Spain and created many portraits of the royal family.

Sofonisba outlived two husbands, both of whom encouraged her to work. When she was in her nineties, she was so famous that other artists traveled great distances to talk with her.

Properzia de Rossi (PROH-per-tsee-ah duh ROH-see) was a famous artist and **sculptor** in her lifetime. Despite this, we don't know much about her today. Properzia was famous for carving tiny sculptures out of fruit pits. Most of these tiny works showed scenes from the Bible in great detail.

Art changed a great deal during the Renaissance. Figures became more lifelike as artists studied the ancient art of Rome and Greece. They also learned to use math concepts, including angles, rays, and lines, to show distance and shape on a flat canvas. This is called linear perspective.

She sculpted large works, too. In fact, Properzia was one of the first women to sculpt with marble. She made a number of marble busts, as well as large altar pieces for churches.

Some male artists didn't like competing with Properzia for work. They tried to discredit her by saying she painted about improper subjects. Some of the church leaders refused to put her work on display. She died at age forty, but she never gave up her work.

▲ *The Chess Game* was painted by Sofonisba Anguissola in 1555.

During the Renaissance, education for women became more common. As a result, more women could read and write. Margery Kempe was a writer, but *The Book of Margery Kempe* was probably copied down by a **monk**. Margery most likely told her story to him.

In the book, the author gives a detailed account of the life of a middle-class English woman. She tells what it was like to have fourteen children. She offers opinions about her marriage and her efforts to start a business. She also describes in great detail her many **pilgrimages**. These are journeys to religious sites.

POINT
VISUALIZE

Imagine you are Margery Kempe. Describe a typical day that you might write about in your book.

▲ Renaissance women often went on pilgrimages.

Most women of the time did not write about daily life. Many wrote about their faith in God. Others urged readers to follow the teachings of the Roman Catholic Church.

A humanist writer named Christine de Pizan (PEE-zahn), however, wrote about social issues. She tried to use her writing to change people's views about women. Christine may have been the first woman to make a living as a writer. She was a widowed mother who wrote to support her family.

▲ Over the course of her career, Christine de Pizan wrote fifteen books.

Sometimes people hired her to produce works. For example, the Duke of Burgundy hired her to write a biography of his brother, the king of France. Other times, she wasn't hired. She would write and dedicate a book or story to a well-known patron. She hoped that the patron would reward her for the dedication.

THEY MADE A DIFFERENCE

In the late 15th century, Cassandra Fedele (feh-DEH-leh) was one of Italy's most famous scholars. She addressed the Senate and spoke at universities. She wrote brilliant letters to fellow scholars. Her bright career seems to have ended when she married at age thirty-four.

Another writer who stood up for women was Isotta Nogorola (ee-SOH-tah noh-GOH-roh-lah) of Italy. In the 1400s, writers often argued about who was most at fault when Adam and Eve were sent from heaven. Isotta took up the question in a series of letters to a well-known humanist and Venetian nobleman, Ludovico Foscarini (loo-doh-VEE-koh FAHS-kuh-ree-nee). She wrote that Adam and Eve were both at fault. Her letters were so well written that she became famous.

Except for medicine, women of the Renaissance did not study science. But women had cared for the sick for hundreds of years. Male doctors did not examine female patients. Women went to midwives and healers for health care.

IN THEIR OWN WORDS

In her poetry, Isotta Nogorola wrote about her "Cyanum." Cyanum was her family's country house near Verona. This poem was written in the early part of the 15th century.

"How often, when I have been seeking learned songs, has it helped me to have discovered the Muses . . . How often has this house opened its doors to men endowed with virtue and to guests sprung from noble families."

▲ This painting by Domenico Ghirlandaio is titled *Birth of the Virgin*. It shows a midwife and her assistant helping a mother at the birth of her child.

Over time, cities began requiring doctors to have studied at universities. Women were not allowed to study at universities. They could no longer care for patients. In 1322 in France, a healer was charged with treating patients illegally. The court decided against her. She had to stop seeing patients.

One woman who contributed to the study of medicine was Alessandra Giliani (JIH-lee-ah-nee). She was an assistant to a doctor who wrote an anatomy handbook in 1316. Anatomy is the study of the human body. She was the first person to begin injecting colored liquids into the body. She then traced where liquids flowed throughout the circulatory system.

CONCLUSION

The Renaissance was a time of learning and change. But for women, the type of life they lived depended on the family they were born into. For the first time, some women had money of their own and used it to start businesses, buy things, or give to the church.

Working-class women worked side by side with men, but women had fewer rights. Even so, they took an active part in the daily life of farms, towns, and churches.

In large numbers, women joined the church. Many women in the church spent their lives helping the sick and the poor.

Women of the ruling class took over duties for absent or underage male rulers.

▲ In this 1499 painting, *Making Butter*, Renaissance women work at their chores.

In the arts, women's roles are harder to define. Many gave up writing, painting, or sculpting when they married.

Women had long played important roles in medicine. They had always cared for the sick and for each other. During the Renaissance, laws changed to make it harder for them to do so.

Still, women remained a vital part of their changing world. Some women of the Renaissance pushed past tradition to create new roles and find new freedom for themselves. Thanks to the women of the Renaissance, women's contributions slowly became more accepted. They helped redefine what it meant to be a woman for future generations.

▼ Today, women of diverse backgrounds are leaders in academics and business throughout the world.

Women in the Renaissance

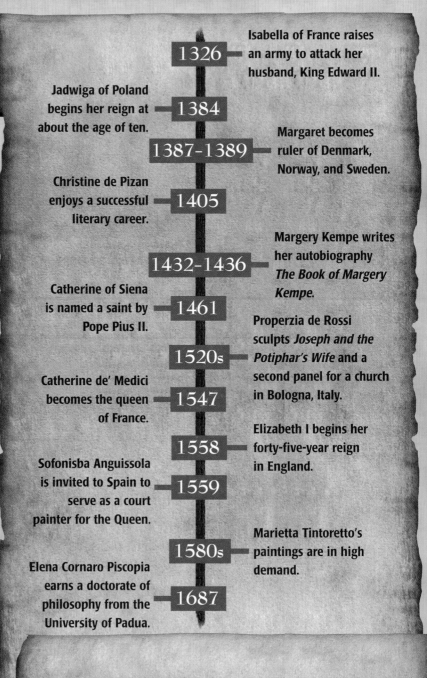

1326 — Isabella of France raises an army to attack her husband, King Edward II.

Jadwiga of Poland begins her reign at about the age of ten. — **1384**

1387–1389 — Margaret becomes ruler of Denmark, Norway, and Sweden.

Christine de Pizan enjoys a successful literary career. — **1405**

1432–1436 — Margery Kempe writes her autobiography *The Book of Margery Kempe*.

Catherine of Siena is named a saint by Pope Pius II. — **1461**

1520s — Properzia de Rossi sculpts *Joseph and the Potiphar's Wife* and a second panel for a church in Bologna, Italy.

Catherine de' Medici becomes the queen of France. — **1547**

1558 — Elizabeth I begins her forty-five-year reign in England.

Sofonisba Anguissola is invited to Spain to serve as a court painter for the Queen. — **1559**

1580s — Marietta Tintoretto's paintings are in high demand.

Elena Cornaro Piscopia earns a doctorate of philosophy from the University of Padua. — **1687**

GLOSSARY

apprentice (ah-PREHN-tihs) young person who works for a craftsperson and learns the craft at the same time (page 7)

city-state (SIH-tee-stayt) city that, together with surrounding territory, is ruled by its own government (page 12)

dowry (DOW-ree) money, land, and other goods that a bride shares with her husband when she marries (page 6)

humanist (HYOO-mah-nihst) person believing that the study of subjects such as art, music, literature, and architecture are key to improving life (page 2)

inherit (ihn-HAIR-iht) to receive something upon the death of a parent or other relative (page 16)

marriage contract (MAIR-ij KAHN-trahkt) agreement in which two sets of parents seal the terms for a future marriage between their children (page 14)

monk (MUHNGK) man who pledged himself to the church and to the service of others (page 24)

patron (PAY-truhn) wealthy person who supports an artist, writer, architect, etc. (page 18)

pilgrimage (PIHL-gruh-mihj) journey to a religious site (page 24)

pope (POHP) leader of the Roman Catholic Church (page 11)

regent (REE-jehnt) someone who acts as a substitute for a ruler who is unable to perform royal duties because of illness, youth, or other reasons (page 17)

sculptor (SKUHLP-tuhr) artist who makes statues from marble or other materials (page 22)

tutor (TOO-tuhr) person who teaches individuals or small groups (page 5)

INDEX